Platform Papers

Quarterly essays from Currency House

No. 6: October 2005

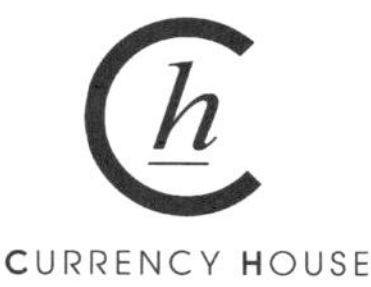

PLATFORM PAPERS
Quarterly essays from Currency House Inc.
Editor: Dr John Golder, j.golder@unsw.edu.au
Currency House Inc. is a non-profit association and resource centre advocating the role of the performing arts in public life by research, debate and publication.
Postal address: PO Box 2270, Strawberry Hills, NSW 2012, Australia
Email: info@currencyhouse.org.au Tel: (02) 9319 4953
Website: www.currencyhouse.org.au Fax: (02) 9319 3649

ISBN 0 9757301 2 6
ISSN 1449-583X

Cover design by Kate Florance
Typeset in 10.5 Arrus BT
Printed by Hyde Park Press, Adelaide

This edition of Platform Papers is supported by donations from the following: Katharine Brisbane, Malcolm Duncan, David Marr, Tony Scotford, Alan Seymour, Greg and Fiona Quirk, Mary Vallentine. To them and to all our supporters Currency House extends sincere gratitude.

Contents

AVAILABILITY *Platform Papers*, quarterly essays on the performing arts, is published every January, April, July and October and is available through bookshops or by subscription (for order form, see page 70).

LETTERS Currency House invites readers to submit letters of 400–1,000 words in response to the essays. Letters should be emailed to the Editor at j.golder@unsw.edu.au or posted to Currency House at PO Box 2270, Strawberry Hills, NSW 2012, Australia. To be considered for the next issue, the letters must be received by 4 November 2005.

CURRENCY HOUSE For membership details, see our website at: www.currencyhouse.org.au

Art in a Cold Climate

Rethinking the Australia Council

KEITH GALLASCH

Author's acknowledgements

My thanks to Mary Travers, Philip Rolfe and Sarah Miller for kindly discussing with me aspects of the Australia Council's relationship with innovation in the 1980s and 1990s. Unreferenced quotations from the three of them are drawn, with permission, from unpublished interviews. Thanks also to Richard Letts for the opportunity to read 'Art at the Edge of Chaos', his report on likely influences on the arts up until 2010, commissioned by the Australia Council in 1994, but not published. Letts' accounts of complexity and other systems theories are applied to the arts with apt examples, including the evolving structure of the Australia Council, regional music organisations and arts movements. My thanks also to the many correspondents over the last year who have generously discussed the Australia Council restructure with me. Sue Blagrove provided welcome comments on drafts of this essay and Virginia Baxter, as ever, offered insight and inspiration. Finally, thanks to Katharine Brisbane and John Golder of Currency House for inviting me to contribute through *Platform Papers* to desperately needed public debate about the arts in Australia.

The author

Keith Gallasch is the Managing Editor of *RealTime*, the national arts magazine focused on innovation in the arts, which he founded with Co-Editor Virginia Baxter in 1994. A former teacher and academic with an MA in Theoretical Linguistics, Keith has been involved in theatre since 1976 (as a founding member of Troupe in Adelaide) and in 1987, with Virginia, formed the performance company Open City, writing, performing and producing new works at Performance Space and for radio until 1996. Open City's performance works include *Tokyo Two* (1987, 1992), *Photoplay* (1987, 1994), *The Girl with a Stone in her Shoe* (1989), *All That Flows* (1990), *The Museum of Accidents* (1991), *Sense* (1993), *Sum of the Sudden* (1993), *Shop & The Necessary Orgy* (Sydney Festival, 1995) and *Promiscuous Spaces: Table Talk* (1996). Keith continues to write for performance and has worked extensively as a dramaturg, developing scripts by Timothy Daly, Jennifer Compton, Dina Panozzo and Christine Evans. In 1997 Keith wrote the scenario for The opera Project's *The Berlioz, Our Vampires Ourselves*, and in 1999 the script for the same company's *Tristan*. He has been a member of the Literature Board of the Australia Council (1983–85), the Board of Management of Performance Space (1990–92) and the Asialink advisory committee on performance (1999–

2001). For the Australia Council he has edited and produced the internationally distributed *In Repertoire* series promoting Australian performance.

Introduction

On 8 December, 2004 the Australia Council announced an internal restructure in the terms proposed by its Future Planning Task Force. Given that the restructure was internal no consultation with clients, stakeholders or the public was offered. Recognising that the proposed internal changes, including the dissolution of the New Media Arts and Community Cultural Development Boards, would have serious external ramifications, artists and arts organisations met across Australia. Protests ensued and new lobby groups formed. Council conceded to consult, but only about how to best effect the restructure. Selected representatives from the new media and community arts fields were invited to meet the Task Force in what were titled 'workshops'. Council formally accepted the proposal to restructure on 8 April 2005.

The formation of the New Media Arts Board in 1996, although not without controversy, was seen as enlightened. Here at last was an Australia Council Board that could formally address experimentation and innovation in the form of the hybrid and new media practices that had been steadily developing over two decades, work that had been difficult to categorise and, consequently, was often neglected or under-funded. In 2005 the board has been dissolved, its 'clients' dispersed to the traditional artform category boards. The subject of this essay is what the demise of the New Media Arts Board tells us about the broader relationship between the Australia Council and the arts.

At a time of great cultural diversity and burgeoning new arts practices which connect unprecedentedly with our everyday lives, it is astonishing that the Australia Council has reversed its own evolution. The authoritarian manner in which it effected this change, the further diminution of the role of artists as peers within Council and the silencing of new media arts—it is no longer represented on Council—sadly parallel the deliberalising of democracies the world over. While there might be enormous diversity on the ground, the ideological push to centralise and to control threatens to yield a monoculture, a condition to which the Australian arts has institutionally been too long inclined.

The arts, ecologically

In contributions to the growing debate about the state of the arts in Australia, I've described the arts as an ecosystem: a self-organising, intricate, dynamic network of numerous agents looped together, competing for but primarily sharing resources, mutually evolving and responding to emerging organisms and innovations, and without a governing consciousness.

What I first thought was a helpful metaphor to wield against the fragmentary and utilitarian view of the arts inherent in the pervasive managerial model of the moment turned out to be more than an analogy. Human systems, whether linguistic, economic or cultural, operate not just *like* natural systems, but in the same way, as self-organising systems, albeit with varying degrees of conscious agency. But we're increasingly aware that theories of economics, for example, don't fit with the actuality of economic systems—economies operate like natural systems, but not like neo-liberal economic theory.[1] Art too is part of our nature. Complex patterns of art production and reception evolve, and mechanisms to manage them. But the manager and the system, like gardener and garden, can slip out of kilter and what was once creative co-operation at the edge of chaos (as one systems theory would have it) becomes dysfunctional, yielding uncreative dis-equilibrium.

A significant manager in the arts system (if now one among many), the Australia Council is not only attempting to wind back the clock of artistic evolution but also to usurp its partners, leaving 'clients' and 'stakeholders' out in the cold. Declaring itself 'leader' of and 'catalyst' for the arts, the danger is that the manager will lock into autocatalysis and use up available resources to keep itself alive. I exaggerate, but you get the picture.

The restructured Australia Council positions itself above the arts ecosystem of which it has long been a part, albeit in an increasingly difficult relationship, its funding levels essentially frozen, its roles and functions multiplying, its structure rigidly top-down, and less and less responsive to the bottom-up emergence of new ideas and forms that regenerate the arts.

Living in paradox

'Living in paradox' is the 2005 title for Ars Electronica. Based in Linz, in Austria, it is arguably the world's leading new media arts festival. This year a prestigious Honorary Mention in the Interactive Arts category has been given to an Australian work, *Intimate Transactions*, created by Brisbane-based artist Keith Armstrong and the transmute collective. Armstrong and his collaborators have attracted the support of the New Media Arts Board of the Australia Council for the development of the work. The honorary mention is a tribute to the Board's judgment and just one example of the success Australian new media art enjoys internationally. In *Intimate Transactions*, body movement, intuition and digital systems merge to bring people together in non-verbal communication over huge distances, maintaining the ecology of human networks in the face of 'techno-fetishisation'.[2]

Describing the hybrid as 'the signature of our age', Ars Electronica 2005 celebrates its pervasiveness in nearly every aspect of our lives.[3] The acceleration of hybridity has been fuelled by globalisation and digitisation: 'With globalisation comes implosion, all cultures and time zones piling up upon each other. When imploding, things either integrate or break. Another driver is digitisation, inviting an infinity of recombinations, all hybrids, carefully cultivated with software, like flowers.'[4]

One of the paradoxes of our age is that cultural diversity, social complexity and constant innovation are countered with an inclination towards the insular and the monocultural. Despite Australia's rich history of new media and hybrid arts reaching back to at least the mid-1970s, the Australia Council has decided to close down a board, formed as late as 1996, that focused its attention directly on these practices. Meanwhile, back in Linz, Ars Electronica 2005 will see the launching of the Ludwig Boltzman Institute for Digital Culture and Media Science, one of the world's largest digital media art archiving projects, with works dating from the Ars Electronica of 1979.

> We talk in Australia about being good at invention, but bad at commercialisation. I think that story is out of date [...] the good-at-invention thing dates from the 1980s. The task now is not to commercialise what we invent, but to try to catch up and to stay in the ranks of the developed world... [Jonathan West][5]

Hybrid and new media arts are part of that Australian inventiveness, but if the Australia Council's absorbing them into traditional artform categories dilutes their standing and their funding, as well it may do, we stand to lose a great deal. We are culturally poor if we cannot live with paradox.

An emerging metaphor

A couple of years ago at Performance Space, a small group of concerned people met to discuss the parlous state of dance in Sydney. Australia Council funding had declined radically, grants were fewer and further apart, and the dance department at the University of

Western Sydney was destined for extinction. At the meeting, Amanda Card, Executive Producer of the dance company One Extra, described the dance scene as 'a collapsing ecosystem'. The phrase stayed with me, and in the ways things do, like self-organising systems in general, I was suddenly alert to the widespread use of ecology as metaphor in many aspects of our lives. But its use was largely casual. I thought I'd try to push it a bit further, but playfully. NSW dance ecology is, by the way, on the mend, thanks to a mixture of vision and pragmatism from Ausdance NSW, One Extra, Performance Space, the Australia Council and especially the NSW Ministry for the Arts, all acting in concert. The result includes Critical Path with its excellent workshop space in Drill Hall at Rushcutters Bay and financial support for short-term project development and international choreographic workshops. Overall funding levels for dance are still inadequate, but the local habitat is much improved. The lesson for the Australia Council's Dance Board is, I hope, that a blanket application of the principle of funding for excellence can, in fact, inhibit growth of excellence in an under-resourced environment.

When I found myself in 2004 protesting the ABC's severely reduced commitment to the arts, I saw the institution as opting out of the arts ecology and expelling the many artists who had benefited from the various niches it had provided—labelled by ABC management as 'ghettos'. Next, publicly available reports commissioned by the Dance and Theatre Boards of the Australia Council gave me the opportunity to analyse the quality of the feedback in the arts system, and to speculate on how a report could fail to comprehend a decade of innovation in dance and so misrepresent the field. When the Australia Council announced its latest restructure, I immediately saw it in terms of potential damage to the emerging and entwined ecologies of hybrid and new media arts. All of this has led me, in this essay, to describe these ecologies, to sketch a history of the Australia Council's response to them, and to place the Council's ambivalent attitude to innovation in the context of the political cooling of the climate for the arts over the last decade.

If you're not attracted to extended metaphors, my apologies in advance. My aim is to replace a limiting set of managerial metaphors, born of neo-liberal economic theory, with another that is open-ended and relates to the way systems actually operate. It can contemplate the very things the managerial model cannot: innovation, emergence, excellence ('best practice' excepted, of course) and history, and do it with nuance and, as Robyn Archer demands, dialectically.[6]

We should never underestimate the power of metaphor to shape our view of the world, each other, and the arts. The linguist George Lakoff has shown the astonishing extent to which we use metaphor to shape our experience.[7] His understanding of it has played a role in forming strategies for countering the right-wing rhetoric that has invaded our lives like a virus and in which the arts are, of course, value neutral and elitist.[8]

The innovating art animal

We are the art species. Stephen Pinker writes, 'Art is in our nature—in the blood and bone, as people used to say; in the brain and in the genes, as we might say today'.[9] Jared Diamond identifies 'the most important innovation that came with our rise to humanity: namely, the capacity for innovation itself'.[10] Elizabeth Grosz describes our hybrid lives as occupying 'the space between the natural and the cultural [...] in which the biological blurs into and induces the cultural through its own self-variation, in which the biological leads into and is in turn opened up by the transformations the cultural enacts or requires'.[11]

For these and other contemporary thinkers, the borders between culture and nature, and between science and art, are dissolving. New media arts reunite science and art after a long separation; the hybrid arts break down artforms we inherited from the nineteenth century. As systems evolve, new elements emerge from within, working their way, bottom-up towards acceptance and, if successful, modifying the whole. The interplay with resource-controlling top-down forces—co-operative or resistant—is a vital part of the life of the system. (The terms 'bottom-up' and 'top-down' can irritate with their insistent sense of hierarchy. Lakoff has much to say about metaphors of verticality and their relationship to the ways we describe our well-being. In this essay, hierarchy sometimes turns out to be the right image, if a problematic one. We are dealing with power.)

Innovation and agency

Innovations emerge from adaptations to crises, from working newly-found materials, new territories, new technologies, new ideas. They search out new niches, or take over existing ones (hence the anxiety in theatre circles in the mid-1990s about sharing funding with 'image-based theatre'). Their presence challenges accepted notions, for example, of form and excellence. They present co-evolutionary opportunities in the form of new partnerships, as the hybrid arts have amply illustrated. They are mimicked and duplicated and so spread themselves. The result in any system is continuity, turnover and renewal, with a developing biodiversity in which organisms share and compete for resources. Some long-lived species stabilise ('heritage arts'), while others are still in the throes of creative emergence ('contemporary practices'). Some species are protected (the major performing arts organisations), some are in need of protection from time to time (contemporary dance).

But what role do we play in influencing and attempting to manage systems that seem to have lives of their own? In his book on artificial life art, *Metacreation*, Mitchell Whitelaw offers the provocation that:

> [...] art gives rise to emergent phenomena (culture, discourses) that inform the production of subsequent works in the feedback loop of ongoing emergence. Taken to an extreme, art could be regarded as a self-reproducing cultural entity, an abstract life form traversing social, biological, psychological, and technological strata.[12]

It could be, but we know that individuals and groups, organisations and movements play roles in determining if innovation is to be taken up or ignored. We know, for example, that we should be able to 'manage' the environment better than we do. Agency is part of these systems, even if no governing consciousness is to be found.

This essay is about the interplay between a set of emerging art practices and the system that has both accommodated and countered it. It is about an organisation within the arts system, the Australia Council, and its attempts to manage that system and its innovations. At the same time it is about individual artists and managers, agents in the system, who have played a role in its making.

Challenging the metaphors that have shaped our lives into business plans and performance agreements has led me to re-think the Australia Council, especially upon recognising the proposed restructure as an anachronistic adaptation, an act of regression and, like previous restructures, an admission of the Council's failure to secure adequate funds for its clients, but a failure for which its constituency will pay.

1 Emergence

> [S]lime mold spends much of its life as thousands of distinct single-celled units, each moving separately from its comrades. Under the right conditions, those myriad cells will coalesce [...] into a single, larger organism, which then begins its leisurely crawl across the garden floor, consuming rotting leaves and wood as it moves about. [...] The slime mold oscillates between being a single creature and a swarm. [Steven Johnson][13]

Are most artists bottom feeders, scavenging the leftovers of the arts omnivores? Do they, like slime mould, comprise a self-organising system producing co-operative, innovative, emergent behaviour? Several significant events drew artists together in 2004: the tenth birthday celebrations of *RealTime*, the national arts magazine focused on innovation in the arts, which I co-edit; the twenty-first birthday of Performance Space, long-term Sydney home to the hybrid arts; and the 8 December announcement of an Australia Council restructure that would dissolve the New Media Arts Board, key funder of new media and hybrid arts, and the Community Cultural Development Board, whose 'clients' also include new media and many hybrid arts practitioners. From celebration and recognition of years of hard work and creative achievement to frustration and despair in a matter of months.

At a forum held during the Performance Space celebration, I read Steven Johnson's graphic description of slime mould to the audience, mindful of the intricate history of interdependence and co-evolution shared by individual artists and companies and the Space itself. The network loops out to and back from PACT Youth Theatre, Urban Theatre Projects, Sidetrack Performance Group, several university departments and numerous individual companies and artists. Beyond that it connects nationally to PICA (Perth Institute of Contemporary Arts) and the partners in other states in the new Mobile States touring project (including the Australia Council, the Performing Lines touring agency and with support from the federal government's Playing Australia touring program). Performance Space and PICA collaborate to produce Time_Place_Space, the hybrid arts laboratory held in Adelaide. It's an annual event that develops vision with the help of leading overseas practitioners. There are hybrid performance niches across Australia nurturing new forms from Hobart to Cairns, from Darwin to Perth and in a growing number of regional centres. Together these discrete creative organisms add up to something more than the sum of their parts. In terms of nourishment most live at the bottom end of the 'small-to-medium-sector' of the arts hierarchy (a chain established by tradition, taste, power and money, and with roots in our evolution as a species), but they constitute a complex system that displays emergent behaviour, working bottom-up to produce innovations of great importance.

Similarly, and with a great deal of overlap with

hybrid arts in habitat, resources and works, new media arts practitioners and organisations form a complex and evolving network. It includes ACMI (Australian Centre for the Moving Image, Melbourne), one of the world's first dedicated spaces for the exhibition of new media art; ANAT (Australian Network for Art and Technology); the Australia Council-ANAT Synapse program, which brings together artists and scientists; Sydney's dLux Media Arts, Melbourne's Experimenta and other exhibitors and nurturers of new media art. There are the many artists and companies at work in the field. There are also the major events that celebrate new media art: MAAP (Multimedia Arts Asia Pacific, held in Singapore in 2004, Beijing in 2002), BEAP (Biennial of Electronic Arts Perth), SOOB (Straight Out of Brisbane), Electrofringe (Newcastle), the Time_Place_Space hybrid arts laboratory, and unsound (Wagga Wagga). Most of these events have international participants. Queensland Art Gallery has trainee new media art curators. In the universities there are many courses and a growing number of degrees in electronic arts, as well as the art-science collaboration, SymbioticA, at the University of Western Australia, and iCinema, innovating in screen technology, at the University of New South Wales with a major Australian Research Council grant. Most of Australia's international film festivals now have dedicated new media programs. The works of Australian new media artists are widely distributed to international electronic art events and internationally admired. Young artists are strongly represented in SOOB and Electrofringe and have benefited from the Australia Council's Run_Way program taking them overseas to exhibit or to investigate new trends. Given the scale and extent of the new media network represented here—and that's without listing the many artists—no wonder then the palpable shock and outrage felt when the Australia Council's Task Force proposed shutting down the New Media Arts Board.

If new media arts is not an artform, as the Task Force declared, it is none the less a field of broadly aligned practices that require artistic sensibility and skills, as well as technical or scientific knowledge and know-how. Like any emerging artform, the practices already involve new tools, new channels of distribution and broadcast, new audiences and new patterns of remuneration, as John Smithies, former head of ACMI, argued eloquently on Artshub Australia.[14]

New media artists engage directly with digital and analog technologies, making complex creations, responding to everything from cell growth to biorhythms, to the weather and the sounds of the universe. They investigate communication, various forms of interactivity, genetics and sensory worlds beyond our immediate perception. A first glance at new media art suggests that it's merely a part of screen culture or just another aspect of visual arts, because its images are often realised on video or computer monitors or other screens. But this is a seriously limited view. New media art includes virtual reality, various forms of interactivity, robotics, bionics, data distribution, bio-mimicry, game-playing, web art and more. Artworks can be in a state of constant evolution, organically or digitally; they can be initiated by an artist and completed by an audience; they can be triggered into action by audience movement, the sounds they make or, as in the work of George Khut, by tuning into their own biofeedback.[15]

New media artworks are themselves often hybrids, building on but transforming existing artforms and technologies, because the digital offers the possibility of endless permutations. Over the last year, workshops for artists in five Australian cities have explored the potential of mobile-phone art, with the phone transformed into a tool for the creation and distribution of art. The often brief works offer video, film, photography, animation, web art and game-playing in various permutations. Large-scale outdoors events utilise networks of collaborating phone-users.[16]

For hybrid art practitioners, mastering and adapting new media technologies or collaborating with new media artists has become vital for facilitating the multimedia and cross-artform work that pre-dated digital applications. This has been developing in Australia since at least the mid-1970s, but has accelerated in the last decade. It has led choreographers, for example, to make interactive installations, digital animations, collaborative dance relayed across great distances, dance with virtual selves, and images of dancer subjectivity. The form remains dance, but it is dance transformed and on its way to other possibilities. The digital in hybrid arts is not just a value-adding extra. Artists are making magic with it and, given the speed with which it has impacted on our everyday lives, helping us assimilate, critique and control its influence.

New media and hybrid arts are doing what new or

revitalised artforms have always done, re-engaging the senses, repositioning us so that we see the world and our relationship to it anew, and changing our relationship with the artist and the art object, which can now be interactive and evolving. In this work there is sensuality, viscerality, a new engagement with body and mind, parallelling a notion of cognition not merely as thought but, as Geoff Davies expresses it, 'sensing the world'.[17] These works are not just about sight or sound, but the relation between our interior selves and the world through touch and smell, our biorhythms, our spatial sensibility, and also what we can learn through the technologies now aiding the deaf and the blind to connect with the world. Then there are the works that once triggered will go on to make further works of their own volition: living art that we can 'garden'.

New forms also offer opportunities to revitalise the way we think, talk and write about art, as *experience,* instead of being locked into thinking about how we think we think about art, or how totally culturally scripted the art experience is. New media and hybrid arts offer surprise, awe, the uncanny, new worlds. We can re-enter the phenomenological loop between audience and artwork in new kinds of participation and collaboration. Prophetically, Susan Sontag concluded her 1964 essay, 'Against Interpretation', with 'In place of a hermeneutics of art we need an erotics of art.'[18] Its time has come.

Hybrid and new media arts epitomise 'living in paradox'. They are the art practices of the moment, generated from the accidents and care of decades of innovation and crafting, emerging bottom-up from the efforts and talent of individuals, small groups, networks, support organisations and nurturers alert to the new. By the end of the twentieth century there were established artists, exhibiting organisations, support networks, courses, major festivals, international acclaim and a responsive Australia Council, in the form of the New Media Arts Board: the ideal of the top-down meeting the bottom-up. What went wrong?

Yes, artists are like slime mould. In a system that loosely self-organises, artists consume the world, in their way, converting it, together and apart, into heightened sensing, both palpable and virtual, for their co-inhabitants. But sometimes, sadly, they are regarded by cultural gardeners as the slime that is offensively not of the natural order of things and must be tidied away. But the more we know about self-organising systems, the clearer it is that managers are themselves part of the ecology, and they do their best when they are responsive to bottom-up developments, otherwise, like monopolies in nature or business, they 'hang on anachronistically and become drags and stultifiers'.[19]

The Australia Council's decision to dissolve the New Media Arts Board represents the destruction of a vital part of the new media and hybrid arts habitat. This at a time when the field is still emerging, when important loops between its discrete organisms are still being formed, when its international reputation is high—overseas institutions and artists were astonished at its demotion—and its potential is strong in the long term for developing markets and audiences.

Feedback: dance hybrids

Let's look at hybridity in one traditional artform category—dance. Here the primary forms absorb techniques from other practices, introduce new media into their productions, work new spaces and change their relationship with their audiences and create new ones. The work remains dance, but in a state of mutation. At one level, this is simply evolutionary, as the interests and passions of a new generation reshape the form. But at another it can be seen as highly adaptive. Dance ecology, outside the largest companies, has consistently appeared to be threatened in Australia for at least the last decade. But that doesn't mean that dance isn't adapting to a difficult environment.

Feedback mechanisms are vital to the well-being of any system. In 2003 the Dance Board of the Australia Council commissioned 'Resourcing Dance, An Analysis of the Subsidised Australian Dance Sector' from the consultancy company Positive Solutions (an ironic title given some of their recommendations). It's full of alarming statistics that reveal the key problem to be a serious decline in funding to dance in real terms since 1992, and worst of all for the small-to-medium sector. The report concludes with a long list of unfocused recommendations, a number of them insufficiently addressed in the body of the report, if at all. Here was a report that couldn't put a precise figure on what was needed, seeking \$3–5 million over 3–5 years and without indicating precisely where it would allocate the monies.

In its investigative criteria, the report ranked 'a healthy dance ecology' second to 'individual excellence'.[20] There was, however, no cogent description of the dance field as ecology. Although it criticised a dance strategy in France as too 'top-down' to be applied in Australia, the report provided no clear model for improving the dance environment from the bottom-up. It was hard to see the point of the report's own top-down, un-costed, extravagant recommendations, none of which addressed the immediate well-being of the sector. They included a second-tier Aboriginal dance company, expatriate dancer residencies, a national dance festival and a dance animateur scheme, all of which were fine in themselves, but not when survival was the issue. There were recommendations that made sense, that would improve the dance habitat: these included improved funding; the streamlining of applications; cohesive dance funding strategies within the Australia Council (a number of Boards and the Audience and Market Development Division spend on dance), as well as between the Council and state ministries; management training; and the much-needed development of producers and presenters.

A set of emergency recommendations were proposed in the event of government failing to come up with additional funding for the sector. These included cutting the number of funded dance artists and companies in an already tiny population by applying the criteria of excellence. In the words of the report, '[S]uch elitism would pass as common sense in Australian sport.'[21] This failure to understand the relative ecologies of sport and the arts reduces the issue in effect to mere competition. Besides, what kind of excellence is to be supported?

Except in the most cursory way, the report fails to address the kinds of innovation developed in dance practice for over a decade. These include the spread of improvisation across Australia as a way of sustaining practice as well as a form in itself; developments in studio practice (Omeo in Sydney); new network support (STRUT in Perth); the integration of sound artists and DJs into performance; the sudden growth in the number of choreographer-filmmakers and the production of award-winning dance films; the creation of dance installations; the successes of dancers with disabilities; the emergence of the dance artist speaking in performance; the absorption of various forms into dance, e.g. physical theatre, aerial performance, martial arts and popular forms like hip-hop; and, above all, the engagement of a large number of artists with multimedia and new media arts practices in an artform hitherto more inclined to the purity of unmediated dance.

Aspects of this transformation are certainly noted in the report, but are not made central to its concerns. The Reeldance film event is described in some detail, but nothing made of it. The report could have proposed, for example, a program of filmmaker-choreographer development through a national partnership. This could involve the Australian Film Commission, Australian Film Television and Radio School (AFTRS), Film Australia, the Victorian College of the Arts, SBS, the ABC, Ovation, state film-funding bodies and Australia's film festivals, and with Reeldance as cultural broker. On the new media front the report could have proposed a long-term strategy to build on Australian dance artists' proclivity for exploring new ways of working with bodies virtual and real through some of the organisations mentioned above, as well as the growing number of new media departments in tertiary education.

The small-to-medium dance sector's integrative response to new technologies, to popular culture and other artform practices, should have been read as highly adaptive behaviour with a potential to engage with a larger and a younger audience and a wider range of resources as demonstrated by Chunky Move, Lucy Guerin Inc. and the Australian Dance Theatre, as well as many smaller outfits. Garry Stewart, the artistic director of ADT, for example, has melded pragmatism and vision in his balancing of urban, regional and international advantages and obligations. The dancers are always acknowledged as co-creators of the work. The dramaturg is seen as a vital and on-going participant. Local talent outside the company is given opportunities to workshop. New works are phased in as works-in-progress and sometimes re-worked in response to audience and reviewer responses—this is highly adaptive. Of course, Adelaide also has Leigh Warren + Dancers, providing competition for funds in a small ecosystem in which all of ADT's activities signal a constant optimising of its immediate environment, while extending its reach with international acclaim for its innovations.

There are, as well, many individuals and companies in dance whose works are innovative and adaptive. But the system is short of creative producers, brave presenters, touring networks and adequate funds to sustain the very practice on which all else depends. The dance report praises the sector for its innovations but cannot make use of them.

In contrast, the report prepared by Ian Roberts, 'An Analysis of the Triennially Funded Theatre Organisations of the Theatre Board of the Australia Council', December 2003, is a more focused and cohesive document, implicitly concerned with the individual and collective well-being of one group of companies, their connections with each other, and challenges from their environment. It treats the sector like an ecosystem, although the metaphor is not used. The report targets business development, improved marketing, co-production and association, touring and dramaturgy. It looks to the best ways for each company to efficiently draw nutrition from the environment, to save energy and to co-evolve (through shared productions and a national association), helping to clearly identify what is competition and what is a resource. The report critically addresses touring—the dispersal of a species in order to find new niches to maximise its potential and its income. It recommends the Mobile States touring initiative and the reform of Playing Australia. It suggests specific funding for much-needed dramaturgical support which addresses the actual work, its very quality. The report sees each company as an organism, but also as part of a complex and adaptive system and it encourages awareness of this. CPI adjustments to funding are recommended so that companies can connect with the overall economic growth of the nation. (The failure of governments and funding bodies to allow for annual CPI adjustments to grants typically belies commitment to the business models imposed on artists and arts organisations.)

Reports provide boards, Council and government with feedback upon which they may or may not choose to act. Clearly the feedback on the parlous financial state of theatre and dance had no impact on our politicians. However, although unable to address fundamental sustainability, both boards have subsequently put into place programs that strengthen infrastructure, expand national and international touring and residencies, and, in the case of dance, address its promotion.

I appreciate that reports are written in such a way as to tell tell bureaucrats and politicians what the problems are and how they can be addressed, but without admitting them into debate about the art—it's an arm's-length strategy. But if the analysis is wrong because the report writer cannot grasp the importance of aesthetic developments, of innovations that could yield additional support for dancers, then what kind of feedback is provided, other than that dancers are a helpless, threatened species? A Dance Board without sufficient peer expertise, without the critical overviews so rare these days in the arts, risks badly misreading its own field. Boards must comprise sufficient numbers of members who have a deep understanding, not only of developments in their own and other forms but also of the hybrids in between.

The Task Force for the restructuring of the Australia Council recommended staff training in the recognition and handling of hybrid arts now that the artform boards are to be directly responsible for them. Those who were invited to consult with the Task Force made the point emphatically that, likewise, expertise was vital as a criterion for board membership. The definition of a peer was weakened in the 1996 Australia Council restructure to include 'persons with an interest in the arts'. Ministerial appointments to the boards are frequently inappropriate. Contemporary art practices and their innovations cannot be nurtured in the wrong hands.

2
Innovation and the Australia Council

Where's a history of the Australia Council when you need one? How can you have a 30-year-old institution with a memory only as old as one of its few long-serving staff members? Without it we develop a collective cultural Alzheimer's. I've had to make do with my own faltering memory and some helpful respondents in order to compile this strictly informal historical sketch of the Australia Council's relationship with innovation.

The Australia Council has always set great store by innovation (it's long been high on the list of criteria for grant-giving). As a consequence, it has supported a great deal of remarkable work over its lifetime—not in every artform and in different ways at different times. But at the level of policy it took a long time to translate this into something as formal as a committee or board focused on innovation. Individual artform boards had their moments of concentrated engagement with innovation, but it was the emergence of the Hybrid Arts Committee in 1994 within the Performing Arts Board, and the more comprehensive New Media Arts Board in 1996 that signalled Council's first overt commitment to innovation outside the traditional artform framework.

In the 1980s the pressure to address innovation came largely from what were called cross-artform practices in performing arts. Such work is now commonly referred to as 'performance'. Performance—or 'contemporary performance', or 'non-text based theatre', or 'image-based theatre'—is an exemplar of hybridity. Emerging distinctly in the 1980s from a pre-history in the avant gardes of the twentieth century, individuals and companies created works for stage, studio, gallery, outdoor and virtual spaces, merging a range of movement and theatrical practices in which spoken text often, though not always, played a secondary role to visual and aural imagery. In Australia in the 1980s the practice was seen in the work of the All Out Ensemble, The Sydney Front, Open City, Entr'Acte Theatre, Lyndal Jones and many others. The categories and criteria of funding bodies in the 1980s and into the 1990s were challenged as this kind of work proliferated. Mary Travers, a project officer at the

Australia Council from 1979 to 1989, recalls that a term often used in the early 1980s was 'new form'.

In the Council's *Annual Report, 1981–82*, the Theatre Board expressed its desire to maintain support for innovation. The 1983–84 report noted:

> [....] unprecedented growth in activity and interest in community theatre, multicutural, black and new form theatre. [...] Those working in new form and other areas maintain that they have not had their fair share of funds—despite the fact that they are commissioning and presenting Australian work, introducing new actors, writers, directors, designers and experimenting with form and content.[22]

Papers about cross-artform practices and the need for committed support appeared in the early to mid-1980s from Mike Mullins (the performance artist founder of Performance Space), Richard Perram (a project officer) and Lyndal Jones (visual artist and performance producer). Mary Travers and choreographer and board member Cheryl Stock wrote a breakthrough paper on Creative Development which was accepted as a funding category in 1984, in recognition of the importance of the collaborative creative process prior to rehearsal.

The *Annual Report, 1984–85* records that, 'to deal more effectively with [...] cross artform concerns [...] Council agreed that 1984 should see the establishment of an Inter-Board committee'.[23] While a member of the Literature Board of the Australia Council in 1985, I sat on the Inter-Board committee. I vaguely recall feverish discussion ranging across community and Aboriginal arts, the tribulations of Australian content in arts festivals and the challenges of group-devised work.

The pressure to find funds for new developments inclined the Theatre Board to reduce funds to major companies, part of a much-resisted trend in the 1980s. The 'ceiling funding' strategy of 1985 was meant to place 'the Board in a position to respond positively to new developments in the art form'.[24] Although well-intentioned, the strategy was mishandled. Julian Meyrick describes it as 'ineffective from the outset [...] aggravat[ing] mistrust between the major and smaller theatre companies'.[25]

In 1986 Robert ('Bomber') Perrier of the Murray River Performing Group boldly proposed a large percentage of grant monies go to 'a fund specifically designated for creative and innovative projects which need not be fully developed proposals at the time of submission'.[26] Andrea Hull, then Director of Policy and Planning, pulled together the key concerns detailed by Mullins, Jones, Travers, Stock and Perram, writing:

> [In] spite of some Boards' attempts to address the need to fund new and risky projects, the Council is still structurally unable to adequately and sympathetically respond to artists who have original and often multidisciplinary ideas, and whose work can't be defined by our existing program categories and criteria.[27]

During the same period there had been a small investment in new media arts. The 1982–83 report features a photograph of holographer Paula Dawson and celebrates the establishment of the Arts and Technology Advisory Committee. Formed in

September 1983, it initiated a series of residencies in partnership with the Australian Film Commission, which placed artists and filmmakers in the CSIRO Division of Applied Physics. In the *Annual Report, 1986–87,* the Art and New Technology Committee reported spending its $36,000 on experimental film and video, new musical instrument development, computerised musical instruments and computer graphics.

It was not until 1989 that a cross-artform funding category was set up within the Performing Arts Board, but it lasted barely a year, falling prey to a complex process of assessment by and allocation of funds from member committees. The *Annual Report, 1991-92* states that '[i]n recognition of a new fusion of artforms the [Performing Arts] Board has agreed that 1 per cent of future funds be ear-marked for cross-artform projects'.[28]

'It was chance and sympathy when it came to funding new work', says Travers of the funding of innovation in the 1980s. However, the work was demanding attention and there were homes for it, niches like Performance Space and PICA (Perth Institute for Contemporary Arts). Sarah Miller has been artistic director of both spaces and in 2004 the Sidney Myer Fund recognised her crucial role in shaping contemporary arts in Australia with a Facilitator Award. She and her predecessors—founder Mike Mullins, Nicholas Tsoutas, Noëlle Janaczewska and the late Alan Vizents—created a milieu of difference and sheer invention. Miller pays particular tribute to Vizents, 'whose papers for Performance Space and PICA on contemporary arts culture "percolated up" into our consciousness of how innovation was being handled, or not' and shaped the trajectory of both PICA and Performance Space.

Miller thinks innovation didn't take off in the Australia Council in the 1980s because 'it was assumed that it would come from the major companies, despite the evidence of the 1970s to the contrary. Innovation in the small-to-medium sector was not recognised.' However, in the early 1990s, with the right conjunction of personalities and expertise a significant change of attitude was about to take place. As Deputy Director of the Performing Arts Board from 1989, Philip Rolfe was to play a key role in this development.

Rolfe is currently Executive Producer in the Producers Unit at the Sydney Opera House, where, since leaving the Australia Council in 1999, he has nurtured an impressive team of producers, transformed programming with the introduction of contemporary and often hybrid works, developed interstate networking and a commissioning program, and, along the way, created new audiences. Travers says that Rolfe 'kept the board's eye on innovative things, helped shape the constituency of the Drama Board and opened up the marketing side of the Council'. Miller also pays tribute to Rolfe for gathering expert opinion about innovation, including the likes of Stephen Armstrong, Tony MacGregor, Teresa Crea and Wesley Enoch, 'very different people, very different backgrounds, but who came together to support unique work'.

Rolfe was Sydney's Nimrod Street Theatre manager in the 1970s and then worked in London, 'where the alternatives to the mainstream in theatre and dance were very strong [...] a whole, viable "other industry", which people took seriously.' His experience of working for five years on international and national arts programs for the 1988 Australian Bicentenary also inspired him, expanding his artform experience and awareness of innovative Australian artists: 'We wanted to pose some serious alternatives, to include things in the programs that people in this country hadn't seen a lot of.'

On arrival at the Council, Rolfe thought that 'there seemed to be a lot of internal support for innovation, but the hierarchy didn't get involved in it [...] Nothing had really imprinted itself on Council that cross-artform work was really useful'. Proposals to formalise funding for it met various forms of resistance, in part because when Rolfe arrived at the Council every board was independent:

> There was never any time to debate the merits of cross-artform work. There was always suspicion about crossing boundaries. It was almost like, 'Here comes a money grabber.' [...] So the amalgamation of the Council into one organisation with one booklet and comparable guidelines was more than a bureaucratic construct, it was a very important device to ensure that there was a meaningful interconnection between boards.

But it was not to be enough: 'It became absolutely clear after a while that bartering between boards wasn't going to get anywhere [...] A new thing had to be carved out to deal with creative development that was by nature non-single discipline.' The result was the Hybrid Arts Committee. Forming it wasn't too difficult,

Rolfe thinks, because by then so much hybrid work was in evidence, including to Council, that it could not be ignored.

What also helped was the existence of the Creative Development funding category created in 1984: it was, as Rolfe says, 'extracted, set up on its own and that's where the Hybrid Arts Committee came from'. The committee was driven by the Theatre Board:

> [...] the most progressive of the three boards. Music was screaming [...] because they didn't believe in it. Dance wanted to believe in it, but always cried poor. Theatre was very generous. Visual Arts never came to the game. Their opinion was that they'd already dealt with the situation and they were light years ahead and they didn't need this approach. So it started as a practice thing, with a committee with a limited life span, making not decisions but recommendations. But once started it sort of snowballed and eventually after 18 months to two years and a lot of backroom policy, and whatever, it became legitimate in 1996. And it had to change its name to New Media!

Rolfe would have preferred to retain Hybrid Arts as the title, but there was strong resistance from 'people who couldn't understand what hybrid meant. I thought it was obvious—and they knew about flowers and gardening.' The appeal of technology for bureaucrats and politicians in the age of *Creative Nation* [29] won out. Rolfe thinks that:

> From that day, right through to when it finished, the board became too bogged down in technology, frankly. It lost its way from what we originally

> thought it could be. The ideal would have been something that dealt with new ideas and new approaches irrespective of the mediums.

As for his role as an agent of change, Rolfe says his attitude was to 'work positively for things that were not strongly represented while maintaining objectivity about what came in the door and how to deal appropriately with it, and to keep reminding the peers of the necessity to do so'.

Philip Rolfe's experiences at the Australia Council point to the complexities of the top-down, bottom-up dynamic. Rolfe and his responsive board and committee members were not at the top rung of Council, but in a position just strong enough, and despite resistance, to read the signs coming from the field and to fashion changes that would grant hybrid and new media arts a niche of their own within the organisation, even if it was never as certain a terrain as had been hoped. Not a few hybrid artists soon found themselves shifting periodically between the Theatre, Dance and New Media Arts Boards in search of just the right niche. It was a modest improvement, but about as good as it would get with funds tightening. For many new media and sound artists, however, it created a new world of opportunity.

Throughout the 1980s and into the 1990s the impediments to support for innovation within the Australia Council comprised a limited grasp of innovation's significance, a struggle to envisage formal means for its assessment and management, and, not least, competition for limited funds, as the major companies attempted to secure their funding niches.

Eventually, the major organisations would find a home of their own in the Major Organisations Board (subsequently the Major Performing Arts Board). But innovation in the form of hybrid and new media arts had at last found its own place in the funding sun.

3
The Death of a Board

Despite various objections, a problematic title and limited funds, the creation of the New Media Arts Board indicated that at last the Australia Council was being responsive to the emergence of new fields of practice, so new in the history of the arts that naming them was difficult, let alone deciding whether or not they were artforms per se. Perhaps the very notion of artform was about to be challenged, as many of us had long expected. Above all there was excitement that the Australia Council had sprouted what could be a much-needed artistic research and development branch. Here was an opportunity to respond consistently to new ideas, new forms and, critically, to the interplay between the arts and the massive changes being wrought by the digital revolution. Artists have been integral to this revolution as inventors, innovators, critics and the creators of new audiences.

Then on 8 December 2004, in a pre-emptive strike—it came without warning, without consultation—the Australia Council announced an internal restructure that would include shutting down the New Media Arts Board, its clients to be dispersed to the Visual Arts/Craft Board and the Music Board, and the hybrids 'triaged' to the most appropriate traditional artform boards. In the months that followed, facing protracted protests, Council opened itself to consultation. The meetings with the Task Force that planned the restructure revealed that there was no comprehensive aesthetic rationale for the dissolving of the board, only the stricture that the practices the board had funded were not artforms in their own right, and an assertion that their presence would instead be regenerative for the artform boards which had not been consistent in their support for innovation. One of the few concessions made was that Council would commission a 'scoping review' on the standing and state of new media arts. But this would be shamefully after-the-event. By not conducting its own intensive review of the New Media Arts Board and the field prior to proposing the restructure, the Task Force abdicated its artistic responsibility altogether.

Plenty of opinions circulated about the reasons for the New Media Arts Board's fate, for example that the board had passed its use-by date, that the field was no longer 'new', that the overlap between New Media Arts Board and the artform boards was now too sizeable to make sense, and that hybrid art and new media art are quite different and have been competing for the same limited resources. These are precisely the opinions that should have been tested with a review and public debate. Opinions are easy and talk is cheap; considered argument is derided in an age of dictatorial impatience and autocratic bureaucracies.

The collective, accrued knowledge of the New Media Arts Board has now been lost. Members of the Board were often faced with proposals requiring them to grasp new ideas and emerging critical languages. Lone experts on new media and hybrid arts will find life even more difficult in the old artform boards, especially the Visual Arts/Craft Board, whose already-extensive purview will have to accommodate yet more forms and acquire more knowledge.

One of the most problematic of the Task Force's recommendations was that 85 per cent of New Media Arts Board funds for new media art go to the Visual Arts/Craft Board on the spurious ground that: 'In analysing the Board's funding patterns we found that roughly 85 per cent of the 'new media' work that the New Media Arts Board supports is in visual media'.[30] Here the 'visual' becomes an impossibly vague category. New media arts practitioners come from many backgrounds—film, biology, communications, physics, architecture, performance, music, sound art—as well as the visual arts. Central to the issue here is the assumption by some in the visual arts that new media art comprises performance, installation, photography, video and little more.

At the meeting of the Task Force with representatives selected from the field by the Council, Visual Arts/Craft Board Manager (now Director) Anna

Waldman reassured us: 'I think you will find that the Visual Arts/Craft Board is your *natural* home.'[31] We weren't convinced. The 15 per cent balance of New Media Arts Board funding has gone to the Music Board for sound art (as New Media Sound Art in the New Work category), a complex field that increasingly entails other artform practices, including the visual.

As for Hybrid Arts grant applications, they can be directed to the artform boards or to the new Inter-Arts Office where they will, in turn, be referred to the appropriate board or, in special cases of categorisation problems and with very limited funds, be assessed by arts peers for funding by the office itself (which will also handle the triennially-funded Australian Network for Art and Technology, Performance Space and *RealTime*). If the Inter-Arts Office does its job well and monitors the fate of applications, it might protect hybrid arts from the inevitable depredations of dispersal. The office needs to provide the traditional artform boards with the critical outside eye that will aid their aspiration for revitalisation. But only if its advice is heeded.

Finally, the redistribution of funds in this restructuring points to a curious anomaly. Given the performative nature of much hybrid art and the adventurousness of the dance and contemporary performance communities in hybrid arts, surely a significant proportion of the funds should have been distributed across the artform boards. Where will a choreographer using new technology now turn to for additional funds required? The Dance Board has no new money for this. All the more reason that there should have been a considered review of forms and needs before the restructure. The CEO's mantra that the restructure was strictly internal and that artists had nothing to fear, did not convince. Despite the claim that there would be continued recognition of new media artists on the Visual Arts/Craft Board, and quarantining of funding in the short-term, it was announced that the two two-year fellowships formerly available each year to new media artists would be 'competitive' with visual artists! Already the habitat was being re-arranged, re-named, artists uprooted and replanted in more demanding terrains at a delicate stage in the development of new practices. Not only that, the species was now mute, without a board it would have no voice on Council.

I like to imagine that had there been an independent review of the New Media Arts Board prior to the announcement of a restructure, it might have recommended enlarging the funds and responsibilities of the board, so that the Australia Council could have become consonant with the greater cultural habitat. It may well have recommended a name change, greater artform board responsibility for hybrid practices, duly negotiated and monitored, and a research and development model of operation. As with the recent Canada Council review of the field, it would have recommended, among other things, seeking out partnerships for securing the additional resources new media art needs.

As a close observer and documenter of the New Media Arts Board's activities and the work it has funded over its short life, I believe that against great odds it has achieved much, both in supporting artists and companies and assisting in the development of new media and hybrid arts' extensive networks. Its mode has been co-operative, its communication intelligent. As part of the arts ecosystem it has been under-resourced, like many of the artists and organisations in its ambit, and it had had to cope with the AFC's substantial withdrawal from funding new media work and the hesitancy of most state governments to commit to these new practices. It had to carry more weight than it could bear. Its abolition amounts to a lost opportunity. The New Media Arts Board could have mutated into a highly focused arena for experiment and innovation.

Why has the Australia Council regressed to an earlier stage of its evolution with the dissolution of the New Media Arts Board? What specific conditions have contributed to this from within the organisation and what attitudes outside it have compelled the decision? Like the universities, like industry—and like them, through research and innovation—the arts have a responsibility to a future Australia. Have we become complacent at all levels about our capacity to invent?

4
The big chill

In the last decade we have experienced a palpable cooling of the arts climate. The public enjoys the arts and attends shows and exhibitions in droves. Art's problems are reported in the media, but its agonies pale in comparison to the crises in health, education, transport, immigration, environment and welfare. Even so, the indifference of both major political parties to the arts in the 2004 electoral campaign—aside from Labor's promise to allocate some additional funding to film—was glaring. What drove the temperature down? Let's go back a decade.

In the mid-1990s a vigorous campaign was waged against the Australia Council by the Australia Council Reform Association, which included artists such as Les Murray and Mark O'Connor, and was supported by sections of the press. Along with allegations of cronyism, artists were consistently portrayed as having their 'snouts in the funding trough' and 'riding the funding gravy train'. The Australia Council Reform Association proposed shutting down the Council, devolving funds directly to established artists and the setting up of the association's own funding committees. The Prime Minister, Paul Keating, appeared to accept their judgment, opining that 'the Council was on the nose' and, in a speech given at the Sydney Institute, the Council Chair Hilary McPhee attacked both artists and the Council's structure.[32] She targeted mid-career artists for imagining the Australia Council theirs, describing them as bitter, feuding and vicious; labelled Council's artform committees 'fiefdoms'; and in the ensuing promotion of the restructure, deployed the populist rhetoric of an 'Australia Council for all Australians'.

McPhee initiated a Council restructure which proposed 'narrowing the gateway' to funding, the introduction of 'buffer zones' between grants, and a diminution of peer assessment (including a redefinition of peer to include interested persons as well as experts). The major performing arts organisations were to have a board of their own, their funds finally secure from the judgment of their species peers. As in 2004, so in 1995 Council had inadequate funds to support its clients and duly turned on them. Council itself had benefited little from *Creative Nation* but rolled with its recommendations to eliminate the expert committees that advised the boards.

The Campaign for a Democratic Australia Council, with the support of hundreds of leading and new artists resisted the changes to peer assessment and challenged the decision that policy-making become the province of Council instead of the result of dialogue between itself, boards and committees. In the end, McPhee promised that artists would remain a majority on Council and the Artform Boards, or Funds, as they were then called. I wrote at the time:

> Really distressing is the way McPhee's rhetoric and her plans for the Australia Council make it a sitting duck for the Liberal and National Party opposition. If you deride a nation's artists and if you turn Council into a machine driven by

economic criteria, it can easily be dismantled in those terms.[33]

None of us was naïve enough to believe that the boards and committees of the Australia Council were saintly, but many of us had sat on them and knew how tough, how exhausting and how scrupulous the process of peer assessment was at most times. The investigative report into the 'White Board Affair' or 'Sports Rorts Debacle' that brought down Minister Ros Kelly praised the Australia Council for the transparency of its funding procedures.

One consolation McPhee offered was that artists would become 'content producers' in the *Creative Nation* revolution. This would presumably help them out of the 'iron lung' of grant dependency, which McPhee described as 'Hugh Mackay's illuminating phrase' (Mackay was on the Council at the time). But artists were not impressed with *Creative Nation* let alone the fact that they were being cast as service providers, cash cows in the new techno-economy.

Not so *Creative Nation*

It's often assumed these days that *Creative Nation* was an artistic vision because Keating was an 'Arts Prime Minister', but it was broader than that, a cultural vision which anticipated the current 'creative industries' concept with its strong vocational and commercial goals. A total of $84 million was allocated over four years, little of it going to artists, although $5.25 million was well spent through the Australian Film Commission when it still had an interest in new media, and $1 million to the Australian Film, Television and Radio School.

I recall a writer in the *Sydney Morning Herald* reporting media industry relief that the 'arts mafia' hadn't got its hands on the funds. Artists found themselves getting short shrift at the costly Multimedia Forums (which had their own budget of $4m) held around the country. The sad thing about all of this was that artists already making significant new media works could have made great partners with the emerging industry. However, they already sensed disaster in *Creative Nation*'s commitment to CD-ROM. As for the much touted Co-operative Multimedia Centres, had they been developed in conjunction with existing screen culture organisations in each state, something might have been seeded other than another sad crop failure. *Creative Nation*, a large investment with a long-term prospect turned out to be disastrously short-term. Like Keating's other visions, *Creative Nation* was admirable, ahead of its time, but inadequately thought through. It was a top-down revolution that ignored the potential already in the system. As for the Australia Council, despite *Creative Nation*, formal commitment to new media art would not be seen until 1996.

Elite outed and ousted

The Australia Council Reform Association campaign, McPhee's assault on artists and the Australia Council itself, and the contradictions in Keating's relationship with the arts nicely complemented the Coalition election campaign in 1996. Artists were labelled 'an elite'. The charge doubtless emanated from a dislike in certain quarters for 'the Keatings', long-term fellowships instigated as far back as 1988 for significant artists, many of them innovators rather than the obvious achievers. It was a scheme which had pretty much run its course by 1996. The attack was also driven by the application of public choice theory, an American right-wing strategy which labels dissenters and minorities as elites. It wasn't long before other 'single interest' groups were isolated by the Opposition. And the role artists had apparently played in contributing to Keating's electoral victories doomed them to vengeance.

Artists were now seen as an elite who'd had the Australia Council wrested away from them. The image of a self-interested minority was to be confirmed by the 'Saatchi' *Australians and the Arts* report which portrayed artists as out of touch with the public.[34] Lumping all arts practices together, interviewing large swathes of the public and a small number of artists and redefining art in the broadest cultural terms, produced an inept report. It has to be asked, to what extent, if at all, the report has been acted on? Its writers thought the arts had a lot to learn from the successes of the wine industry. The analogy was uninspired, and now seems more than a little ironic, given that the Australian wine industry has been criticised internationally for dumbing down with 'industrialised farming' and other economies of scale that are having a negative impact on the markets of the country's small, quality producers.

It's unlikely these events of the last decade greatly impinged on the public consciousness but they did confirm a growing gap between the Council and its constituency, and consequently between artists and the government. Doubtless they did nothing to encourage government to increase Council funding. The increases that did come later by way of the Nugent and Myer Inquiries were generated by forces outside of Council and propelled by arts organisations coming together in common cause.

Cooler and cooler

The globe warms, but the new managerial language of funding is cool. Progressive Council restructurings freeze artists out, their representation as peers sorely reduced in acts of downsizing which diminish the 'gene pool' of arts knowledge in the Australia Council. There are patches of warmth for individual artists and particular productions, or for the contribution of the anonymous many to the 2000 Olympics opening ceremony. There are the arts festivals of Robyn Archer and Lyndon Terracini that innovate the festival model and reach new audiences. But there is little comprehension of the arts as a totality—long gone are the days when arts journalists would write regularly about the state of the arts or report on artform developments. These days it is the profitability of an arts festival that will be uppermost in a journalist's mind, not its qualities or distinctive challenges. An increasingly vocationalist approach to arts training, the banning of compulsory union membership in the universities (with its inevitable impact on the arts) and the sharp reduction in university teaching jobs for artists, all these add to the chill. The ABC's disengagement from the arts has pushed artists further out into the cold, and its 'arts by stealth' strategy (don't mention 'arts'—audiences don't like it!) dropped the temperature to an all-time low.

Climate change is most evident in the limited interest in the arts from the major political parties, who, since the 1980s have looked pretty much the same, sharing neo-liberal principles and a wariness of vision and long-term planning. This is not good for the arts, especially when compounded by the crude Darwinism enacted everywhere by neo-liberal economics, its accompanying, pervasive managerial language, reality TV (in its countless manifestations of survivalism), and a manipulated fear of the Other, above all the refugee—as if suddenly we lived in fear of invasion and takeover. A return to 'island Australia' represents a failure of the imagination which, we always hope, art will correct. Numerous small theatre and performance companies, writers, filmmakers and visual artists have in recent years tried to break the drought that refuses the Other—the refugee, the enemy—an interior life. Our much-vaunted sense of mateship and egalitarianism has been reduced to 'a fair go' for only those who share our most immediate interests. Our empathy has dissipated. We have become emotionally cold.

An ecosystem functions via the many loops formed between its organisms. These represent highly co-operative exchanges of information and resources. A change in conditions, internal or external, can destroy loops. The loops that link the arts with the universities, the ABC, the Australia Council and the federal government have been steadily cut over the decade. At the same time the funding for basic arts resources, for survival, has seriously diminished in real terms despite state governments attempting to make up the difference. New loops forming with the corporate sector (e.g. through the Australian Business and Arts Foundation) and private philanthropy are slow to form, less systematic and come with conditions that will not necessarily favour innovation, let alone provocation.

5
Breaking monopolies

Diversifying resources and manufacturing has not been an Australian trait: the result, agricultural and mineral monocultures. It's not dissimilar in the arts, where large omnivores consume most of the resources. The difference, however, is that they are rarely exportable; they are stay-at-homes. Even the national companies, Opera Australia and the Australian Ballet, move about very little. Meanwhile individual artists and small companies disperse to find new niches here and overseas, embodying work that is idiosyncratically Australian and widely applauded. But they are kept poor, so that the cultural ecosystem remains predominantly a monoculture. The omnivores become, in Tim Flannery's terminology, 'exterminator species': 'they are best at utilising and securing certain nutrients and can out-compete and destroy all similar species'.[35]

The big performing arts companies play a diminishing role in shaping the future of our culture. But they have strong defences: continuity, scale, the glorious plumage of marketing and publicity, high social status, large staff, diverse resources, carefully built constituencies and high per-seat subsidies. This is not to say they are safe from competition (commercial productions, arts festivals), but they will be protected even when they falter. They are rarely co-developers, except from time to time with each other across state borders. On the other hand, medium-sized companies fuel them with a high percentage of new talent.[36]

Could it be that the Major Performing Arts Board skews the functioning of the Australia Council? Within the ecology of the Council, the Board is self-contained, operating on quite different criteria from the artform boards, where peer assessment is critical, where quality, purpose and, often, originality are paramount. The major performing arts organisations are treated as if they are not part of the greater ecologies of dance, music and theatre. They are assessed as businesses. Meanwhile, the gap between these large companies and the rest of the performing arts field simply grows and grows.

What if Council were to be relieved of the administrative and financial burden of servicing these organisations? If the federal government, in co-operation with the states, were to directly fund the major performing arts companies, would that allow Council to focus on the majority of its clients and the key issues in the arts?

An introduced species

The Australia Council intends to introduce another species, 'large-scale projects', into the system to prove to government 'that art can make a difference' and therefore warrant a funding increase that will flow on to the artform boards.[37] The budget of $9 million for the projects represents the takeover of the artform boards' intiative funds. In a radical departure from the model of Council as responsive to the arts ecology, the new artform board directors will seek out projects rather than respond to grant applications, and then compete for funds from the full Council. Although Council has not indicated what kind of projects it has in mind, at a public meeting with artists Jennifer Bott mentioned the possibility of investing significantly in one community, rather than spreading funds thinly across a number. Are we to see something like the adoption of Richard Florida's fashionable vision of cities and communities revived by the creative class who are, in turn, entertained by lesser creatives who provide the pollen of attraction to a city?[38] Art is only an attractor and a by-product in the Florida vision. If these big projects do not have their roots in the existing arts ecology, if their goals are functional, they will become an invasive species, throwing the system out of kilter. And the Council will have assumed another role, that of producer with its Councillors as peer assessors. More aberrations introduced into the system.

Like the large companies that the Australia Council invests in and which absorb most of its funds, the Council itself is behaving like a monopoly. Economic theorist Jane Jacobs writes that 'Nature abhors a monopoly. [... I]nstitutional monopolistic enterprises are often [initially] quick, bright, intelligent, daring and creative', and also focus investment. But 'they all end up dumbed down, elderly and hard to get rid of.'[39] And who invests in the Australia Council beyond recurrent funding? Neither Labor nor Coalition governments.

The climate for the arts might well improve if the Australia Council focused all its energies on the artists, companies and organisations outside the major organisations, and with funding, as Robyn Archer has argued, at least equivalent to that spent on the major organisations.[40] The justice of that equivalence is confirmed by the report on the triennially-funded theatre companies. Collectively they play to as many people as state companies, with a greater geographical reach and almost equivalent sponsorship; but they come cheap at the price and many are facing serious financial difficulties.[41]

Breeding independence

One possible way that Council can reconnect with the arts ecology is to devolve more of its funds, so that it becomes less a grant-processing machine and more and more encourages the growth of creative producers, distribution networks and consortia. I am not recommending that that funds should be devolved through major organisations or state governments, but directly to the small-to-medium arts sector. After thirty years of development surely the arts are sufficiently mature to be able to embrace this.

A significant, if at this stage modest, example of this and an important development for hybrid performing arts is the Mobile States touring program within Australia. It's an initiative of the Theatre Board with contributions from the Dance Board and the former New Media Arts Board. Mobile States is operated by a consortium of organisations and venues across Australia among which are PICA, Performance Space, Brisbane Powerhouse, Salamanca Arts Centre, Arts House (North Melbourne Town Hall) and Performing Lines and, in the latest tour, includes the Darwin Entertainment Centre. Theatre Board Manager (now Director) John Baylis told me in 2004, 'what it tours is the consortium's business, not the Theatre Board's [...] These venues collaborate anyway so Mobile States formalises and builds on that'.[42] Mobile States enriches and expands the habitat for companies and furthers the development of independent producing, presenting and touring. This is nurturing by the Australia Council's artform boards of existing bottom-up potential. It's admirable because, like the best of the Council's relationship with the arts it is collaborative—between boards and with the field. It positions the Australia Council inside the arts ecology, not above, not outside it.

6
Re-thinking the Australia Council

I spent several hours recently reading the Australia Council Annual Reports of the 1980s and early 1990s. Excitement at the recollection of wonderful works created over the decades was tempered by the palpable frustration of Council Chairs at inadequate funds and the challenges of repeated restructuring (in response to both fund shortages and the impositions of various extra-Council reports). Once installed the restructure is usually acclaimed, as it was in 1995 and again in 2005, for making the organisation more 'flexible', a euphemism for 'reduced' and, these days, 'authoritarian'. At each stage, the impression is of an organisation in adaptive mode—negative, because it has to downsize to make do with less; maladaptive, because it makes a wrong move; or anachronistic—it regresses to an earlier form.

It's time to re-think the Australia Council. Increasingly, artists have had to adapt to the Council's limitations rather than Council responding to an evolving Australian arts ecology and to the cultural transformations Australians are living through.

What if...?

Is it time for the Australia Council to shed some of its proliferating roles? As I have already suggested, the major performing arts organisations could be directly funded by the federal government in co-operation with the states. Although in the arts ecology there are some loops between large and smaller companies (with an innovator like Melbourne's Malthouse close to the hub of the ecology), there is none within the Australia Council.

Would the Audience and Market Development Division be more effective as a discrete body? It has much, much more work to do internationally and could galvanise current ad hoc partnerships between government agencies if it had standing and independence. Above all, it could address the neglected development of markets within Australia. The clarification of its role is now all the more critical given that, retitled compromisingly as Community Partnerships and Market Development Division, it has had to absorb the functions of the former Community Cultural Development Board, although exactly how it will do this has yet to be resolved.

Should the responsibility for the projected large-scale Australia Council art projects be given to the artform boards? Shouldn't Council maintain arm's length distance from funding decisions involving the creation of specific works of art?

Although now titled an agency, like other government instrumentalities, should the Council be required to behave like one in its administration of government initiatives (including NOISE, with its tenuous links to the arts ecosystem) and discretionary spending (as with the $5 million that Arts and Sports Minister Rod Kemp directed the Council allocate to the Melba Foundation from the 2004–05 federal government budget)? Shouldn't Council rather focus on the demands of its charter and its own programs?

The foundation of the Australia Council was predicated on the implementation of the arm's-length principle, keeping government at a distance from the arts. It's a principle that has been more or less maintained against sometimes considerable odds. However, one area in which the Minister has unfettered power is in the appointment of Council and artform board members. The expertise of these members is increasingly in question, especially in their ability to understand and assess innovation. Has the time come, as has been suggested for the appointment of ABC Board members, for an independent committee to be established to select Council and artform board members strictly on the grounds of expertise?

I'm asking here what the Australia Council could do for the arts, if its attention and energies were focused entirely on what is commonly called the small-to-medium arts sector, which in my estimation is central to the well-being and future of the arts in Australia and their standing internationally.

Of course, to answer this question adequately would require a comprehensive and detailed review of the sector, one much more thorough than the 'Small to Medium Performing Arts Sector Report' of 2002.[43] The new review would also assess the value of the artform structure of the boards of the Australia Council; the relativities of the funding of heritage and contemporary arts practices by those boards, Music for example, where the new is poorly served; the practicalities of devolving funds to creative producers and various consortia; the role of peers in policy development; and, above all, it would address the need for formal mechanisms to deal with innovation. An assessment of the financial state of the sector and its long-term needs would be a central concern for such a review.

But will funds for a newly focused Australia Council, one integrated with the arts ecology, be forthcoming? The funding increases resulting from the Nugent Inquiry into the Major Performing Arts and the Myer Contemporary Visual Arts and Craft Inquiry suggest that governments will respond in certain circumstances and to certain pressures, and certainly from outside the Australia Council. However, there is a widespread belief that arts funding will continue to diminish. This takes the form of a fatalism which resolves into yet new ways of carving up the same funding cake, or the belief of the Chair of the Australia Council, David Gonski, amongst others, that private philanthropy will outstrip diminishing government funding and corporate sponsorship. Recently interviewed, Gonski said, 'Handel had his patron, who asked for a fugue or a cantata.' The reporter responded, 'Was it tailored to a benefactor's demands?', Gonski replied, 'Perhaps, but I can live with that.'[44] But can artists live with that? The prediction of decreasing government funding for the arts is not merely that of a realist, it's the belief of an ideologue who, although he sees a place for continued government funding, is committed to the growth and prevalence of private sector funding. Australia Council CEO Jennifer Bott and Gonski have declared that they are staking their careers on the large-scale arts projects that will convince government that the Council warrants additional funding for the arts.[45] Can this be believed if its chair 'expects government contribution to the arts to diminish'?

A last word about words. I hear that the Australia Council has decided to stop using the phrase 'small-to-medium arts sector'. Depending on what it's got in mind as an alternative, this looks like a wise move. While accurate in identifying the relative size of its individual inhabitants compared with the major organisations, the phrase fails to convey the sheer size of the sector. It does nothing to acknowledge its energy and diversity, and the fact that it is the breeding ground of talent and innovation. It is the future. For the moment, put aside the bottom-up and top-down metaphors that are invaluable in thinking about how systems evolve, and let's think about the individuals, companies and organisations that constantly renew the arts. Let's see them as being central to the arts ecosystem, however far they are dispersed within it, however established or emerging. A visionary government and a responsive Australia Council will want to make the unhindered well-being of this centre their responsibility.

So, is my vision of unencumbered, empowered contemporary arts practitioners emboldened by hybridity and new media and fostered by a pared-back, purposeful Australia Council nothing but the green dream of an arts fantasist exercising an ecological obsession? Well, like feedback in any system, it's only as good as the use you put it to. Stay in the loop.

Endnotes

1 Jane Jacobs, *The Nature of Economies* (New York: Vintage Books, Random House, 2001); Geoff Davies, *Economia: New Economic Systems to Empower People and Support the Living World* (Sydney: ABC Books, 2004). Social and economic theorist Jane Jacobs, in *The Nature of Economies*, and geophysicist Greg Davies, in *Economia*, demonstrate that economies and cultures are adaptive, complex, self-organising systems operating 'on the edge of chaos' and in which innovation is the driver, as opposed to the linear, equilibrium and 'supply and demand' model of classic economic theory. Their observations are rooted in a co-operative model of Darwinian theory.

2 See Greg Hooper's review, 'The ecology of interaction', *RealTime* 67, June–July, 2005, p. 26; Keith Gallasch, 'Interview: Keith Armstrong. Interactive futuring', *RealTime* 59, February–March, 2004, pp. 21–2 or www.realtimearts.net

3 Gerfried Stocker, 'Hybrid-living in paradox', Preliminary program, *Ars Electronica 2005* (Linz, Austria), p. 10.

4 Derrick de Kerckhove, 'Hybrid-living in paradox', Preliminary program, *Ars Electronica 2005* (Linz, Austria), p. 11.

5 From an edited version of his Deakin Lecture, 'Designing the Future or Tempting Fate', *Sydney Morning Herald*, 11–12 June 2005, 'Spectrum'.

Jonathan West is co-director of the Life Scientist Project, Harvard University and founder of the Centre for Innovation, University of Tasmania.

6 *Myth of the Mainstream*, Platform Papers, No. 4 (Sydney: Currency House, April 2005).

7 George Lakoff and Mark Johnson, *Metaphors We Live By* (Chicago: University of Chicago Press, 1980).

8 *Don't Think of an Elephant, Know Your Values and Frame the Debate* (Melbourne: Scribe Publications, 2004).

9 *The Blank Slate: The Modern Denial of Human Nature* (Harmondsworth: Penguin, 2002), p. 404.

10 *The Rise and Fall of the Third Chimpanzee: How our Animal Heritage Affects the Way We Live* (London: Vintage Books, 2002), p. 43.

11 *In the Nick of Time: Politics, Evolution and the Untimely* (Crows Nest, NSW: Allen & Unwin, 2004), p.1.

12 (Cambridge, Mass.: MIT Press, 2004), p. 227.

13 Steven Johnson, *Emergence: The Connected Lives of Ants, Brains, Cities and Software* (Harmondsworth: Penguin, 2002), p. 13.

14 www.artshub.com.au, accessed 20 December 2004.

15 See Kate Richards, 'Let the body navigate: Kate Richards talks to electronic artist George Khut', *RealTime* 66, April–May 2005, p. 31 or www.realtimearts.net

16 See Anna Davis, 'Mobilising phone art', *RealTime* 66, April–May 2005, p. 28 or www.realtimearts.net

17 *Economia*, p. 220.

18 In *Against Interpretation* (New York: Dell Publishing, 1996), p. 14.

19 Jacobs, pp. 35-6.

20 'Resourcing Dance: An Analysis of the Subsidised Australian Dance Sector', February 2004, p. 5.

21 *Ibid.*, p. 63.

22 *Australia Council Annual Report, 1983-84*, p. 81.

23 *Australia Council Annual Report, 1984-85*, p. 24.
24 Ibid.
25 *Trapped by the Past: Why our Theatre is Facing Paralysis*, Platform Papers, No. 3 (Sydney: Currency House, January 2005), p. 33.
26 Papers, One Day Policy Meeting, Australia Council, 29 April 1986, p. 8.
27 Andrea Hull, 'Innovation—A Working Draft', 28 April 1986, p. 2.
28 *Australia Council Annual Report, 1991-92*, p. 25.
29 *Creative Nation, Commonwealth Cultural Policy* (Canberra: Commonwealth of Australia, October 1994).
30 Jennifer Bott, Australia Council email, 23 December 2004.
31 New Media Arts Workshop with Future Planning Task Force, Australia Council, 22 March 2005.
32 'Creative Tension', *Sydney Institute Papers*, 7. 4 (Spring 1995).
33 'On the road to where?', *RealTime* 9, October–November 1995, p. 3.
34 *Australians and the Arts: Overview. A Report to the Australia Council from Saatchi and Saatchi Australia* (Surry Hills, NSW: Australia Council, 2000).
35 *The Future Eaters: An Ecological History of the Australasian Lands and People* (Frenchs Forest, NSW: Reed New Holland, 1994), p. 93.
36 'An Analysis of the Triennially-Funded Theatre Organisations of the Theatre Board of the Australia Council', December 2003, p. 7.
37 Jennifer Bott, Public meeting arranged by ANAT, *RealTime* and others, Paddington RSL, 24 January 2005.
38 *The Rise of the Creative Class* (North Melbourne, Victoria: Pluto Press Australia, 2003).

39 *The Nature of Economies*, p. 117.
40 *Myth of the Mainstream*, p. 26.
41 'Analysis of the Triennially-Funded Theatre Organisations of the Theatre Board of the Australia Council', December 2003, pp. 8–9.
42 Unpublished interview, 17 September 2004.
43 'Report to Ministers on an Examination of the Small-to-Medium Performing Arts Sector, prepared by a working party of Cultural Ministers Council Standing Committee', March 2002.
44 Lauren Martin, 'Their world away from their office', *Sydney Morning Herald*, 29 July 2005.
45 Lauren Martin, 'Arts body defends axing of positions', *Sydney Morning Herald*, 9 December 2004.

Readers' Forum

Anthony Buckley on our schools' insularity

Storry Walton presents an interesting perspective on the current problems of our Australian industry in *Shooting Through: Australian Film and the Brain Drain* (Platform Papers No. 5). But I don't think the brain drain has anything to do with the present navel-gazing crisis of Australian cinema. A respected writer friend recently had the gruelling task of assessing over sixty Australian scripts. The writer noted that the scripts were for drugs slash movies (boys) or destructive sex slash abusive parents (girls). And that's it. These writers have only two stories to tell until they're 45! And they have invented an entirely new genre called 'I don't read or watch television'. I would add, 'or go to the cinema either'.

You can bring back all our peers and I will tell you it won't make a scrap of difference. In fact I would go so far as to say it would be a great waste of money. The problem lies in the teaching at our insular and cocooned film schools—all of them! Bruce Beresford, Tim Burstall, Peter Weir, Donald Crombie, Ken Hannam et al didn't go to film schools. They learned their skills and craft where it matters—at the coalface, just like those marvellous television directors and writers who went overseas in the 1950s and 60s.

I find Storry's comments on training, under 'Thespian Germs' (p.43), very relevant. Discipline is sadly missing in today's learning equation. One learns more about anything if one has a 100-foot roll of film to learn with (and that's the only roll they're going to get) as opposed to the un-discipline of filming endless hours of tape. Help!

The brain drain from Europe and Britain to Hollywood from 1910 to 1940 didn't stop the growth and development of their film industries. World War II may have, though Britain produced some of their finest films in those dark days of the war. Let actors and artisans go over to Hollywood, the Americans have always recognised new blood. It is our job to create and foster our talent here. Bring back our expatriates if you want, but this is not the answer to our problem, it is the deep-rooted insularity of our film schools in not having supported vigorously attachments and apprenticeships to our coalface practitioners.

Robert Connolly on the dangers of Hollywood

Storry Walton's Platform Paper *Shooting Through* addresses many of the key issues facing the Australian film industry, particularly the impact of 'the global circular migration of talent' and subsequent brain drain. While there is much to be gained from the return to Australia of the talented directors that reinvigorated our industry in the 1970s, I wonder if the current impact of the lure of Hollywood also needs further scrutiny.

In last week's *Sydney Morning Herald* ('Aussie made movie *Stealth* panned in US', 31 July 2005) the international critical response to the Hollywood Studio action film *Stealth* was given particular attention. The film was shot in Sydney with the usual mix of Australian cast and crew in minor roles, and the article inferred that this failure was somehow tied to the crisis in our local industry. After months of unrelenting criticism of our local industry, the media savaging of *Stealth* was perhaps presented as evidence that our industry can't even maintain a reasonable level of quality in locally made studio product (I would have thought *Mission Impossible 2* was already evidence of this). There is, of course, a considerable difference between having a film industry in Australia and the significant value of a strong Australian film industry.

Hollywood has in recent years developed an insatiable appetite for talent, regularly seeking out new directors for its remakes, franchise sequels and summer genre fodder. A damaging trend among emerging filmmakers in Australia, particularly evident among the makers of short films, is a more calculated ambition to pursue such a career, resulting in a diminished standard of work. It is therefore no surprise that the work of the Australian Film Commission's indigenous film unit, and the talented pool of filmmakers it is supporting, have become one of the industry's successes. These filmmakers have a story to tell and an uncompromising ambition to be bold, innovative, and original in the telling of it. To survive now, our industry will need to be driven by these filmmakers and others like them. The focus on a career path to Hollywood is in the short term a dangerous distraction from the main game.

I'm sure Weir, Beresford and Noyce would all agree that the Hollywood that now beckons is very different from the one that gave them the conditions to make their early films outside Australia; and that the ability to finance the cinema they want to make has deteriorated, as has the quality of work available. No doubt they would also agree that the future of our industry now depends on a new generation of filmmakers driven by the stories they have to tell, rather than by any ambition for success in the Hollywood studio system.

Contributors

Anthony Buckley

Anthony Buckley, AM, is a film producer of features, TV and documentaries. His features include *Caddie, Bliss* and the recent success *Oyster Farmer.* Television includes Bryce Courtney's *Jessica*, this year's Logie winner for best mini series, *The Potato Factory* and *Heroes' Mountain.*

Robert Connolly

Robert Connolly is the writer-director of *The Bank* (2001) and *Three Dollars* (2005); and producer of *The Boys* (1998), *The Monkey's Mask* (2000) and the forthcoming *Romulus My Father*.